YOU MIGHT BE FROM MANITOBA IF...

Dale Cummings

MacIntyre Purcell Publishing Inc.
194 Hospital Rd.
Lunenburg, Nova Scotia
B0J 2C0
902-640-2337

www.macintyrepurcell.com
info@macintyrepurcell.com

Printed and bound in Canada by Friesens.

Library and Archives Canada Cataloguing in Publication

Cummings, Dale, 1947-, author
You might be from Manitoba if... / Dale Cummings.

ISBN 978-1-927097-60-1 (pbk.)

1. Manitoba--Social life and customs--Caricatures and cartoons. 2. Canadian wit and humor, Pictorial. 3. Comic books, strips, etc. I. Title.

FC3361.3.C85 2014   971.27   C2014-905535-8

MacIntyre Purcell Publishing Inc. would like to acknowledge the financial support of the Government of Canada through Department of Canadian Heritage (Canada Book Fund) and the Nova Scotia Department of Tourism, Culture and Heritage.

FOREWORD

This is Dale Cummings' love letter to Manitoba. It's a celebration of the peculiar details about Manitoba known only to those who have lived with her.

For a guy who's constantly grumbling abut the harsh winters and the flat terrain and the mud, it's odd that Dale still lives in Manitoba. His problem is, he loves this place.

A lot of people have the same problem. We know all the things we hate about Manitoba, but you can't get us to leave. We get our boots stuck in the Manitoba gumbo. We keep talking about leaving, but year after year, we're still here.

Dale and I have been enjoying Manitoba's oddities and grumbling about them together since the early 1980s. That was when I returned to my birthplace after a few years in Montreal and Ottawa. That was also when Dale left his southwest Ontario roots behind and resettled on the Prairies. The late John Dafoe recruited both of us to write and draw for him on the editorial pages of the *Winnipeg Free Press*. We won our National Newspaper Awards the same year. Dale found room for his household, his studio and his cats, dogs and horses on a farm in Meadows, on the northwestern outskirts of Winnipeg.

For 30 years, Dale has been collecting Manitoba images, living the life of Manitoba people and drawing the caps, the boots, the cars and trucks, the eagle feathers and the coats by which Manitobans recognize each other. In the cold months, you may see a half-ton truck from the Interlake with a cardboard carton flattened against the grille to keep the wind out. Then you know to look for the other Manitoba marker – the extension cord wound round the hood ornament and the external mirrors for plugging in the block heater at night.

Plenty of us have left Manitoba, because it's a small province in a big world. We take those memories with us – the flavour of smoked goldeye, the careful attention to the weather in spring when the rivers might flood, the huge amazing skies where you can watch a summer storm approaching or drink in the great wash of colour as the sun sets, the snow geese briefly crowding the fields as they pause between Texas and Churchill.

The fur traders ran this place for a long time and kept European settlers out. As soon as Canada took over and put a railway through, the settlers poured in because the soil and moisture were good and the harvests were usually abundant. Winnipeg's boom years ebbed as Calgary, Edmonton and Ottawa grew faster. The Ukrainians, the Mennonites, the Aboriginals, the long-established Scots, the lately-arrived Filipinos and many others settled down to live peacefully together in this happy oasis of sanity. We invented the annual Folklorama festival to express our pride and joy in watching each other's ethnic dances and tasting each other's ancestral cooking. We probably didn't invent multiculturalism, but we figured out how to make the most of it.

Everybody knows about the Guess Who and the Royal Winnipeg Ballet. If that defines us for the wider world, that's OK. But we Manitobans also have some secret handshakes, some ways of winking to each other. Let Dale Cummings remind you of a few of them in his love letter to Manitoba.

— *Terrence Moore, Winnipeg writer and editor*

INTRODUCTION

Well, right off the top, I apologize if your favourite peculiarity is not in the book. Limed time, space and talent preclude their inclusion. As for what is in the book, I can only promise that it will never happen again.

As this book is not a one man show, I would like to spread the blame around. First I would like to thank my publisher, John MacIntyre, of MacIntyre Purcell Publishing Inc. for getting me to do this book. At least I think I thank him. I would most certainly never have thought up this much work on my own. And John, I am sorry for the blown deadlines, grey hairs and the nervous breakdown. I do hope you recover.

My thanks as well, to my friends and colleagues, Terry Mosher and Mike Deadder for a well-placed, encouraging boot, where it did the most good.

Terry Moore, Jim Carr, and Gord Sinclair Jr., my thanks to you for taking the time to come up with all the fine words. And Gord, thank you again for getting right behind this cart and putting your shoulder to the wheel.

Many Manitobans sent suggestions that proved to be helpful. I thank you. And thanks to Manitoba itself for all the good material. It's a goldmine.

Thanks as well to friends and relatives for their ideas and suggestions.

And of course, and last but not least (to coin a cliché, which in itself is a cliché), a very special thanks to Jeanette for all her help, her skills as a "learn as you go" computer jockey, and all her forbearance while learning to live with a lunatic. Without her help I'd be blowing another deadline.

Thanks Jeanette,

— Dale Cummings

YOU MIGHT BE FROM MANITOBA IF...

....You are here.

... you got one of these to go get the groceries.

... "garbage mitts" are a whole lot better than they sound.

... you cried when the jets left.

... you cried when they came back.

...this cap is reserved for socials, weddings, funerals,
and everyday use only.

...the crocus is the first sign of spring.

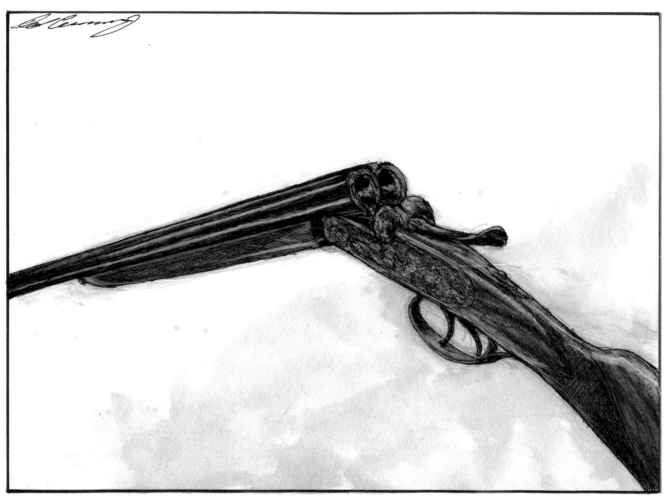

... this is a "tool" not a "weapon".

... that's no *terrorist* ... that's just *Bob.*

... you can say "Hurry Hard" with a straight face.

... you have gone to the far edges of the "Fringe".

... this guy's hanging in your hall.

... you ever had a pair of these.

... winter, sometimes, just hunkers right down on ya.

... you know what a "nip" is.

... the other one's still in the gumbo.

... you've taken up an outdoor activity to beat the winter "blahs".

... if every grouse, no matter what kind, is called a "chicken".

... you live in the "Slurpee capital of the world".

... you remember the Gimli Glider.

... you think a snake pit is a *good* idea.

... you've waited 8 months for this guy to show up
with your morning coffee

... you can pass it around.

... you can bust a move.

... you are a connoisseur of the classics.

... you mourned the closing of Kelekis.

... this is either "stark beauty" or "bleak starkness".

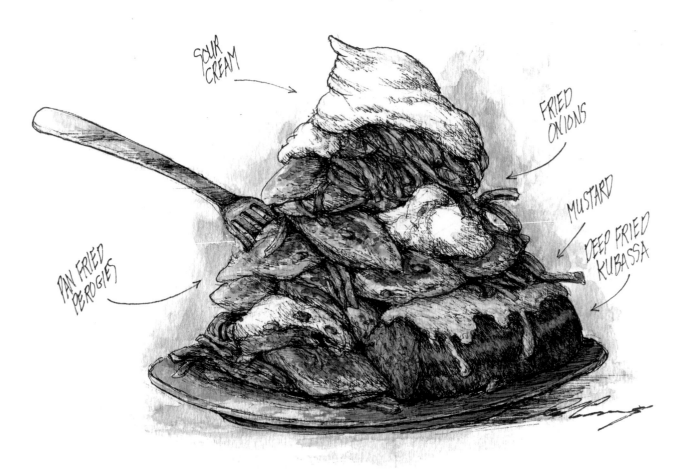

... this is a sort of "soul food".

... you know how to fry baloney so it doesn't bubble and curl.

... you are fiercely proud of your heritage.

... you know who the real Winnie the Pooh is.

... your wallet contains 2 old social tickets and 6 leftover beer tickets
from the one you just attended

... this is not an "electric truck".

... this has nothing to do with breakfast cereal.

... you can identify the "national bird" of Transcona.

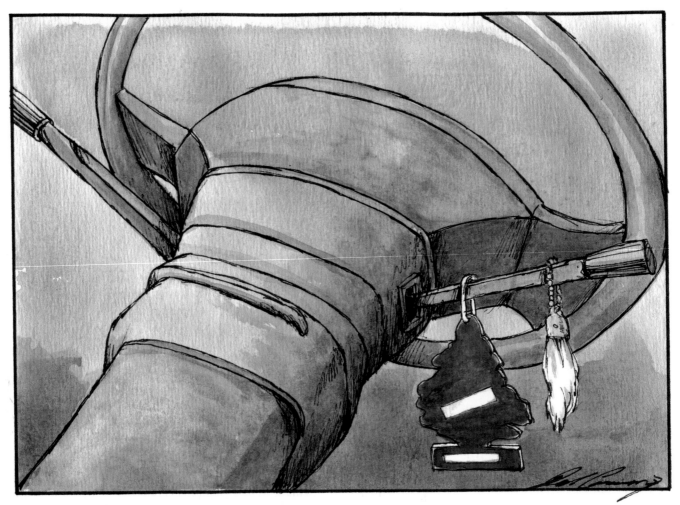

... you've ever wondered what that little stick on the left hand side
of your steering column is for.

... you call jelly doughnuts "jambusters".

... you go fishing every May long weekend and wonder...why?.

... you ever drank "swish" from an old Seagram's barrel.

... you ever had a "booter".

... you know what the hell this is.

... this is your windshield in August.

... you have attended every Winnipeg Folk Festival since the dawn of time.

... you got pelicans.

... you've packed for February.

... you know the meaning of "24.5 feet James".

... you've ever danced the "Red River Jig".

... this is your growing season.

... you know Ice Road Truckers aren't just some guys on television.

... you have this... reoccurring... nightmare.

... you're a cool hand with a bag of Spitz.

... every lump on the landscape is called a mountain.

... you can see a whole freight train all at once.

... you know there are all kinds of potatoes, but you only just like the red ones.

... this is a favorite roadside attraction... the corn as well.

... "surf's up!" in February.

... this requires no further explanation.

... you live where fahrenheit meets celsius at 40 below.

... some days you just don't know where to set the thermostat.

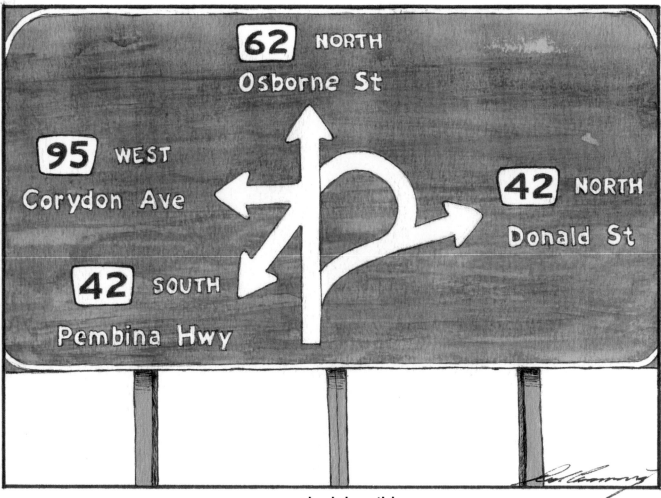

... you can decipher this.

... the kids are "cool", whatever the weather.

... the "windchill factor" becomes a moot point.

... you monitor the daily "mosquito trap count".

... you and your dog both wear tick collars.

... you've been up to take a look around.

... the canker worms are doin' the "Tanglefoot Rag".

... you have a "freight-load" of history.

... you've enjoyed the ice sculpture at "Festival du Voyageur".

... you have augered through 3 feet of ice to hit 3 inches of water.

... this is a frequent destination.

... summer is in bloom.

... you're gonna make it up to Churchill one of these days.

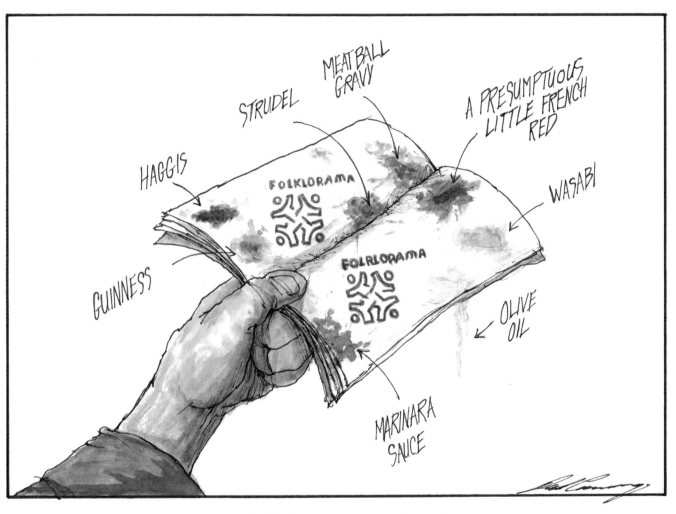

... you've had your passport stamped.

... you get your liquor from the "LC" and your beer from the "vendor".

... you're off to the rodeo.

... you know that the distance between you and an all out
mosquito seige is about "2 1/2 inches".

... you've barbecued in the snow because... "It's April, Dammit".

... you may have noted a certain urban/rural divide.

... you're crawling through the Minus 30 exhaust-fog.

... you would rather *one* of these was *not* "smoked".

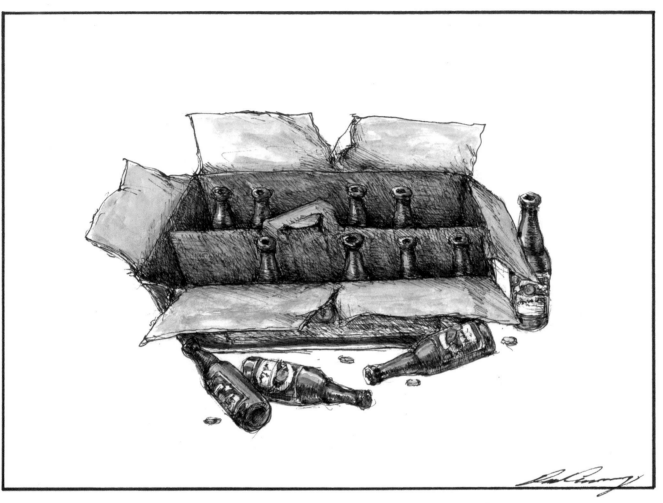

... you've had certain "standards".... several of 'em.

... you don't leave home without it.

... you live in "next year country".

... you reserve the right of criticism for yourself.

Canada's most famous intersection is... well... you know...
...just what they say it is...

... you're still waiting for rapid transit.

... you're set to take on winter... again.

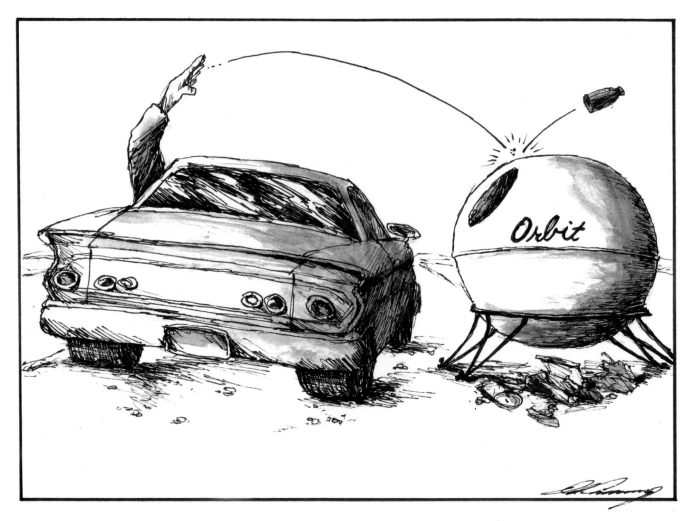

... you've ever launched your trash into orbit.

... sometimes you don't have a lot to say...
because you don't want to let all the warm air escape.

... you've had hands on experience with black ice.

... you have high hopes for the future.

... you've got the Mint, but not the money.

... you're hoping somebody gets the point.

... you were there.

"... south about a mile and a half... then due west at the old Dingle place..
...if you pass the hog barns, you've gone too far." ...
...is a direction you can follow.

... you think your road might be a "Designated Heritage Site".

... the question of the day is... "has the plow been through yet?".

... you got good neighbours to bail you out.

... this is how Santa Claus gets around.

... you lost it in the caraganas.

... you managed to duck the first F5 tornado in recorded Canadian history.

... you have golfed with the geese.

... Duff's Ditch is no "small thing".

... you ever met someone at the Timothy Eaton.

... you rubbed his toe for luck.

... you can appreciate the patch-work.

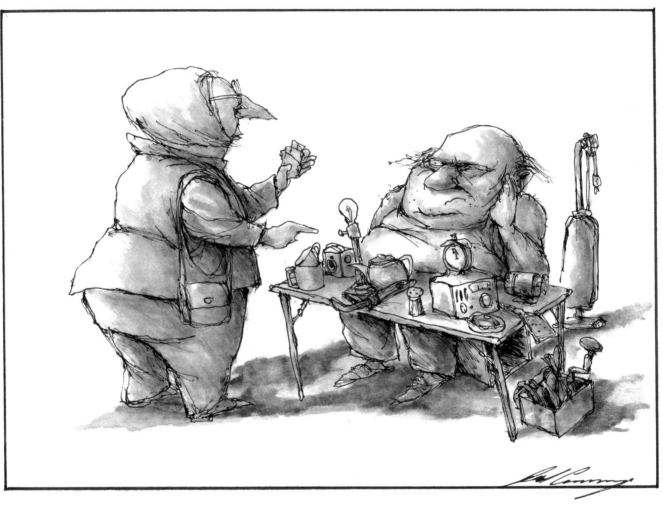

... you clip coupons to yard sales.

... you know why it's called "Valour Road".

... in a good year you might find a Lady's Slipper in the ditch.

... you're off to the Community Hall with a bowl of "pot-luck".

... it's sundown on these old "prairie sentinels".

... you have possibly, the world's greatest collection
of super-sized lawn ornaments.

... three pickups and a combine is "grid-lock".

... it's a fine day in the fall and it doesn't matter if the ducks show up or not.

... sometimes, you think the geese might be smarter than you.

... this is "gittin' 'er done".

... this is pretty much what the place looks like...
not counting the mosquitos, wood ticks, blackflies and blizzards.

... you keep most of your fishing tackle at the bottom of the Lockport Dam.

... this is where you go when you die.

... you're glad to see that the halfway tree is still right there
where it's supposed to be.